How To Improve Mental Health

From a depression and asperger syndrome survivor

Tim Price

chipmunkapublishing
the mental health publisher

Published by
Chipmunkapublishing

http://www.chipmunkapublishing.com

Copyright © Tim Price 2013

Edited by Aleks Lech

ISBN 978-1-84991-956-2

Chipmunkapublishing gratefully acknowledge the support of Arts Council England.

Author Biography

I was affected by lack of Oxygen when I was born and was first diagnosed with a mental health problem in 1990 it was called Depression which people can develop several different kinds of Mental health needs issues or problems they may need the experience of medical staff in hospitals like the Priory, Leighton, or Macclesfield.

I later discovered that I had Asperger's Syndrome.

I received help from staff with experience of mental health issues.

Recovery took a long time with help from hospitals, carers from the Mental Health Unit, my friends and family.

I am normally a positive, happy person and I join in activities whenever I can.

This book is published in memory of my friend, Jane Bowyer, who I went to school with, and my Uncle Tom, Uncle John, and Jason Smith, a good father to Heather and a good stepfather to Charlotte Price. Memories are essential to keep on remembering people.

Activities

Activities to improve mental health

Over the years I have tried lots of activities to help me with my mental health issues and the following notes help explain   the way the activities   have improved my mental health.

Meeting and getting to know different people with mental health issues and experiencing and meeting new ones who join the service and the resources that improve mental health and knowing different staff and members who help improve my mental health further and keeping in touch with them if possible.

The use of sport in general in improving mental health

The practice of sport in general and the use of exercise like going to gyms, swimming, tennis, and other different sports are ways of improving mental health.

Cricket

Cricket was first invented over the centuries and different countries play each other like the Ashes, England verses Australia, men and women cricket teams; the cricket world cup is being held now. We beat Australia in Australia for the first time since 1987.

Cricket is a way of improving mental health, like Marcus Trescothick, who was a very good cricketer and batsman. I enjoyed listening to test match special when he was playing for England against different cricketing nations around the world. The world cup is essential to finding out who is the best cricketing nation every four years. I am also looking forward to test match cricketing nation for the first time. It will be very exciting and enjoyable to find out who it is.

I have been involved in watching various forms of cricket, from Sandbach /Elworth, my local teams, to Test Matches at Old Trafford. All have been enjoyable and have helped me a lot.

Swimming

For many years I have gone swimming to different swimming baths and swimming in the pools on holiday. It improves my coordination and I swim very fast. I used to swim for a swimming club in Sandbach on a Monday evening every week and I go swimming at Crewe baths. I have met different staff over the years and I am very friendly with them.

I think that we will gain a lot of golds in swimming at the Olympics games in London 2012 and really do very well next year at the Olympics in London. I hope to watch the cricket.

This involved going to galas in various times in the local area.

Football

Watching different football fans, and watching football matches to improve mental health is a very important part of the recovery process to watch their local team play different teams in the football league and in the League cup, the Premier League and the Champions League, which are a very important part of football family.

Teams like Crewe Alexander, Manchester United and Manchester City and other teams play each other over the season and also other football teams form the football leagues and create the possibility of playing football in Europe and around the world.

Football is a way of improving mental health and the people who develop the needs and problems over the years and is a way of continuing their improvements and is a way of helping the football teams around the country and the world.

I have been to watch Crewe Alexander, my local team, on many occasions, usually on my own, sometimes with my dad or Uncle Tom. I support Manchester United and have been a member for many years. We go to Old Trafford every season.

Olympic Games

People's mental health would be improved if they took part in more exercise in general, like team sports and the Olympic Games.

These will be held in London in 2012 for the second time in recent Olympic history. The first time was in 1948, the first time the games were held after the 2nd World War. It was important to hold the Olympic games in London in 1948 because it was the first international sporting competition held after the war had finished.

It will be a great experience for me to see the athletes from all over the world competing in London at the Olympic games in 2012. I will really enjoy watching on television a great way for Britain as a nation to hold an international competition, as the whole world can promote complete togetherness against the threat of terror.

It is a way to deter terrorists at any time in the future by any other international competitions to be held around the world.

I am a member of Fitness First

Hockey

I am a supporter of Fodens and Sandbach Hockey club. When I was younger when my dad played Hockey home and away each hockey season against teams, like Buxton,Congleton, and Alsager hockey clubs, I really enjoyed meeting different people over the years playing at different hockey grounds around the country in Wales, England and universities around the country home and away. I enjoyed doing the oranges at half time at home each fortnight, one week at home and one week away from home. The different hockey Clubs had different ways of catering for after the match. This has finished. I really enjoyed watching the hockey games when Sandbach played or Fodens played different hockey clubs around the country and in Wales. I enjoyed been honorary fund-raiser for Sandbach hockey club, raising money for the matches each year, and meeting different hockey players each year.

Snooker

I really enjoyed watching Steve Davies and Tony Meo play each other at the Spectrum Arena at Warrington. They played snooker in what was the called the Mercantile Classic which Steve Davies won. I used to watch Steve Davies and Bill Werbenick play each other at the Lada Classic. Bill used to buy several pints of Lager each frame to relax himself.

The use of Services

The services which are an essential part of improving mental health and the use of resources which people and organisations in the mental health section of the National Health Service provide offer a good way of using funding to meet mental health needs and problems and people who develop them can overcome their problems in time with the right sort of help and guidance in what people set out to do and can achieve with the medical staff and the caring facilities provided for with the amount of funding provided.

The services people receive can be made and people who use them as a way of improving mental health and the use of resources and more funding is made available for the services provided.

So the funding can be spent on different departments in the National Health Service.

Medication

The use of certain prescribed medication and the use of pharmacies around the country and the world like the cooperative in Crewe and around the country the importance of taking the medication prescribed by the consultants or doctors in your own doctors surgery is an important way of improving mental health and the diagnosed mental health issue or problem over the year. Mental health needs or problems will gradually improve over time by taking the right amount of medication . If you can achieve it try to come off medication, but it might not work at first, but you can try again some time in the future. The main purpose of coming off medication is not to rely on it for the rest of your life if possible, and eventually try to succeed without it and make sure that when you try again you succeed the second time with help from your consultants who have helped over the years. If you can be given the chance to try without it at all.

Medication helps you recover from the mental health issue or need or problem but it has to be yourself and you have to try to have the determination to make it succeed and continue with life without medication. An important way of improving mental health, motivation is an important part as well to make it succeed and continue with everyday life without the medication or tablets at all.

My experience of working with Andrea Cameron

I have known Andrea Cameron over the last eleven years. She has looked after my mental health needs and helped me gain more confidence over the years. This gives me the ability to achieve what I have difficulty in achieving with help from other people who I know and get to know over the years and the future.

Holidays

Cornwall holiday

When you visit Cornwall and the surrounding area it is very picturesque and beautiful and very enjoyable to see the sea which is made of different colours. The places around Cornwall and the villages are very nice.

Charlestown is very nice with the sea and the

boats. It is very relaxing to be on holiday. It sometimes rains and it is sunny as well sometimes.

The town of St Austell is very nice and beautiful and very enjoyable and the sea looks very exciting and colourful and you can paint pictures around Cornwall and its surrounding areas.

I really enjoy seeing family and friends in and around St Austell in Cornwall. I make new ones each year. Going to Cornwall can really improve mental health because of the beautiful scenery and surroundings.

Canal holidays

Canal holidays are very important to the tourism industry and as a part of improving metal health and also part of trips as part of services like Link and Macon House. I really enjoy going on the canal; it really relaxes me and I go to different places around the canal system.

The canals were first built by navies and there are several different navigations, like the Shropshire Union, Leeds and Liverpool Canal and other canals on the system and there are lots of pubs to go to.

There are different villages along the canals and boat lifts like the Anderton boat lift which is in Northwich.

The canals were first built by James Brindley and other canal engineers around the country.

They were built before the railways which were the end of the waterways as commercial carriers.

They were an important way of life with the horses pulling the boats to start with.

The Harecastle tunnel is near us in Stoke on Trent. Brindley built the first one and Thomas Telford the second one a few years later, because it became a bottleneck. Boats were pushed through the first tunnel by legging and the horse led over the hill.

The way in which the canals are now used are for pleasure.

The canals are a way of improving mental health.

I have been on lots of canal holidays over the years, starting in 1981 when I went with my brother Robert, my mum and dad, my Uncle Rod and Aunty Pat and their two daughters Joanne and Anita. On the four counties ring we repeated the experience in 1982.

We liked it so much we went again in 1983 and we eventually bought our own boat, a small cruiser called Picador.

In 1993 we brought our narrowboat called Slowcoach, and we have been on lots of holidays including to Nottingham, Wigan, Whaley Bridge, Chester, Llangollen, Worcester and also Birmingham.

Holidays abroad

People who have mental health needs or problems visit different countries around the world. People can book a fortnight or a week on holiday. People go swimming ,walking, and also do other activities around the world.

I really enjoy going on holiday abroad. It relaxes me and it gives me the time to meet new friends and get to know them over the holiday and keep in touch with them if possible.

Holidays abroad are a way of improving mental health, and helps people with mental health and their needs or problems.

It can give them more confidence in achieving their goals.

The Canary Islands

The Canary islands are a very important way of improving mental health, like Tenerife, and Gran Canaria near Spain. The buildings are white to reflect the sun in the day.

The Tenerifian people are very nice and it is easy to talk to them when you meet them.

I really enjoy going to the Canary Islands. I have mentioned it as it is an essential part of improving mental health needs or problems by flying on a plane to the two islands.

The food is very different and you can enjoy your food when it is prepared on holiday. You can meet different holiday makers and make friends with them and keep in touch with them if possible.

Going on holiday is a way of improving mental health needs or problems with the scenery and the surroundings.

The area they work in when you meet are people who are called holiday reps who can help you, settle you into your destination and holiday the day after you arrive.

The Beaches

The beaches around the country and near the seaside and also abroad and the world in different countries like Spain, France, Canada, America and Africa vary with different beaches around the countries I have mentioned as a way of improving mental health needs or problems and also helping people with the diagnosed mental health needs or problems with help from qualified medical staff and the ability to listen to the person who needs to talk about what they need to mention or is concerned about in everyday life and helps the person to recover more quickly so that the person can eventually go into the community after being in hospital.

Beaches can be a way to improve mental health by listening to the birds, the seagulls, and seeing boats in a harbour near the sea around the country and the world.

They are near the seaside with different colours. Some are yellow and some are white and they vary around the world.

You can relax near a beach when you are watching and hearing the waves come in and you can paddle in the sea and make sandcastles on the beach with your family and friends.

Beaches are a very good way of improving mental health.

The use of Link Holidays

Link Support Service members have gone on holiday over the last fifteen years to different places like the Lake District, Wales, Bangor Youth hostels and other places to go to like different countries like France, and Cornwall and different places to go on holiday around the country and also the world.

People with mental health needs or problems can be used to defeat people's general outlook on mental health.

I have met people over the years and made friends with them over the years and I will continue to do so all my life.

The holidays are a way of improving mental health.

The World

The way to improve mental health is to promote the issue and funding and the services and resources available around the world as well for the future generations of people who come into the world now and in the future. The use of international mental health issues and resources which are available to the person who can at any time in their life time access them. The importance of MIND and the mental health charities around the world is to help promote complete independence of mental health services and resources now and in the future, It is as essential now as when it was first discovered and the services and resources are available to the recovery process and the future.

The friends and members and staff work well together in coming out and improving mental health and the world and the future worlds to come.

The Music Industry

The music industry is a way of improving mental health and is an essential part of promoting mental health by singing a song or recording albums by certain different artists around the world and the music industry as a whole.

I enjoy buying records, compact discs and listening to my favourite artists who sing my favourite music like Duffy, Kylie Minogue and Simply Red. These are some of my favourite music recording artists.

Music can inspire you to recover and helps you to recover from several diagnosed mental health needs or problems. It can be make you recover faster and relaxation is important to use in the recovery process and it helps people to improve their lives as well.

I have been to see Kylie at the MEN Arena on two occasions and plan a third!

Reading

The National Health Service offers services in mental health and how to look after the person who develops mental health issues and the use of the services available to them and the resources and the experience of the medical staff who specialise in mental health issues and make friends with patients and people who come into the community and are out of hospital.

The use of people learning about mental health and how they develop in the first place and can recover well depending on background and how you are told the diagnosed mental health issue.

Reading books on mental health can improve the public awareness and help people with mental health issues and also help their recovery further and faster.

Teletext

The use of teletext is an important part of media. It

can be used as a way to promote ideas of improving mental health and the general outlook of people who do not know anything about the services and resources mental health staff. It can provide knowledge of how mental health is provided and the provision is used to finance the staff and people who work in mental health.

It can provide advertising space to promote mental health needs and problems which can help make people become more aware of the services and the country and also the world on world mental health day which is held in October each year.

It can be used by people who do not buy newspapers or listen to the news or newscasters each day of the week.

The National Trust

People who have mental health problems or issues can visit national trust places of interest around the country like Tatton Park, Lyme Park and the gardens near to Little Moreton Hall near Congleton. People enjoy walking around the estates in national trust properties around the country and Britain. People come from all over the world to visit the places and properties.

Going around the properties is a way of improving mental health and is a way to relax and enjoy the scenery and buildings around the country and new ones when open.

The parks are really big to walk around in the country.

Being allowed to visit the properties with people with mental health issues, needs, or problems can promote mental health in general and gives the public an insight of what can be achieved with a person who is diagnosed with the issue and the national trust can help to provide the buildings and properties for people with mental health issues with family or groups and also help the person's recovery. It also helps to promote the national trust organisation, which helps people with mental health issues and they recover faster.

Railways

The use of the railways over the centuries are very important like Crewe Works, Crewe Station and surrounding railways stations around the country in Cheshire and near towns and cities next to Cheshire. The importance of the railway age was an important part of industry and it is important to keep the use of transport going and improving after the canals. The invention of the railways and the use of transport in general is important.

The use of railways can improve a person with mental health needs or problems over time and can improve a person's mental health life and also improve mental health in general.

Theatre

There are different theatres in and around the surrounding areas like the Lyceum in Crewe and the New Vic, in Newcastle Under Lyme and the Regent in Stoke on Trent. These are the three main theatres near to me and my family and my friends. I really enjoy watching different things at different theatres and in different places. I like going to out to the theatre with Link and other places of interest.

I really enjoy going to the ballet, plays, concerts, and Queen tribute bands within the three different theatres in the surrounding area.

They are enjoyable and exciting to watch.

Going to the theatre is a way of improving mental health.

Mental health

The use of mental health and its uses in improving its own subject in the general outlook on itself and people use them to its ability and people enjoy themselves doing things with people with mental health needs and problems. It is an essential part of the service and use of resources that people can learn about mental health at any time they like to experience it.

The use of resources in the funding of the patients or people with mental health needs: it is a very important way of combining the two together when required if needed.

Mental health is a way of improving the above subject and is essential to the learning process and helps people with the above needs in mental health as itself as a subject or focus.

I think that it serves the focus and can could really help people understand the subject easier and make sure it improves mental health.

The big issue with mental health problems

People who sell the big issue sometimes develop mental health issues over time and can start to recover from mental health issues which people can be told they have by the consultants who diagnosed mental health issue, need or problem . The recovery process which people use like services and resources in mental health, can improve lives and the patients or person who is in the community and the people can help with the experience of mental health issues. The way to recover from them is with help from members of staff working well together.

Services and resources

The most important things about improving mental health are the service and resources that are provided by the provision and funding of the whole National Health Service in general and the amount of the department of health provides the service, an amount of millions to spend each year. It is a big policy of which government is in power in the time of its invention in 1948. The way to improve mental health is to fund it where appropriate and use the funding when it is needed to get the most from the millions each year to fund its services and resources.

The state of funding of mental health services and the use of resources that help to run it by talking to staff and members of a mental health centre and also main offices like Macon House. It is an essential part of the service and an excellent use of resources.

The combining of services and resources can really improve mental health in general.

Christmas

The festival of Christmas is an important part of the church year which celebrates the birth of Jesus, the son of God.

We celebrate Christmas by dressing up in the nativity each year on Christmas day which is the 25th of December; by putting up Christmas trees up in the house, in churches and also Christians sing Christmas Carols. Services are held during the month of December. The lead up to Christmas is called Advent. It celebrates the Christmas Story. Christmas is an important time for people with mental health needs and it helps them to recover from their mentioned need. The festival involves sending Christmas cards to people we know and also people we have known over the years and also get to know over our lifetime.

Christmas is celebrated by Christians around the country every year in December. We do our Christmas shopping each year for each other, buying Christmas presents for family and friends. It is important to give as well as receive the presents people buy each other around the world.

Christmas is celebrated in other countries. Some people go away for the Christmas fortnight on holiday and celebrate it in another country for a week or for two weeks, depending on how long the holiday is booked for and transport like planes, caravans and other means of transport to the destination for the holiday to commence and be enjoyed.

Homeless People

Some people become homeless because of circumstances of rent arrears and can develop mental health needs or problems which require qualified help from staff with mental health experience.

This can vary from different towns or cities like Manchester and around the country and the world.

The charity Mind helps people who are homeless and the treatment is available with mental health workers based in Manchester who also make a difference to the homeless persons' lives in general.

Supporting people who are homeless can help people into their own homes and get help that they need to look after them.

The services and resources they require to keep them off the streets and also to help them with everyday life can be a way of improving the person who is homeless to improve mental health and their own lives. It can also be an inspiration to them as well.

Easter

The festival of Easter is a celebration of Jesus' resurrection from being put the cross and it celebrates him rising from the dead on the first Easter Sunday. I really enjoy sharing things with my family and friends I get to know over the years and everyday experiences I gain with help.

The main point of Easter is Easter Sunday, by celebrating the resurrection of Jesus and the receiving of Easter Eggs to family and friends.

I really enjoy Easter time by sending out Easter cards to people I know.

Mental health history

Over the centuries people have developed mental health problems, issues or needs with different kinds of developing mental health. There are services that provide the help when required and the resources that are currently being used around the country and the world.

I hope that we find a way to the best advantage and the funding possible.

Resources are being used to their advantage over time and also improving mental health which has provided part of the National Health Service and also the funding of improvement and the services points and policies of the time and centuries and provision of improving mental health and the potential of dealing with all mental health needs and also in the future.

The combining of all services in combating mental health in general is a long goal which can be achieved and also making sure it does not exist and money can be spent on other National Heath

Services and the use of the resources in the National health Service and is also by using the available funding to continue to improve mental health.

People who inspire me to write this book.

The people who have inspired me to write my book called Improving Mental Health are Duffy, Kylie Minogue and Simply Red. These are some of my favourite recording artists who record music albums.

Mental health and the future.

The state of mental health in the past started in 1601 with the Poor Law. It changed many peoples lives and the general outlook on mental health as a whole. It changed over the years and combined the use of services and resources in the use of mental health patients and people in the community, and other mental health organisations and mental health services around the country and the world. I hope that we find compete extinction of mental health needs or problems in the future. The use of families in combating mental health is also an essential part of the recovery process.

Some people don't have families to talk to , but they can still talk to people with mental health experience and members of staff within a mental health centre or someone to talk about an issue to do with their diagnosed mental health need or problem.

People with mental health needs and problems.

When you first develop mental health needs or problems they can occur at any time during your life. This can be when you least expect them to happen and you may need hospital treatment or you may require it at the time and the services and the use of resources of mental health provision and the experience of members of staff who tell people who have not any experience of it at all.

There should be be more funding made available for the service and the use of resources in mental health buildings and also future buildings in the community.

You may gain experience from a person who has a mental health problem or need and learn from them and improve your own life by knowing them through life and you may meet them at any time in everyday life. With the knowledge of their diagnosed mental health problem they can help you if you develop the need or problem yourself at any time in the future with their own experience of their diagnosed mental health problem or need by talking to you about it or by a leaflet or going to your GP who may refer you to hospital if the need is essential. You can use the experience of the medical staff and other patients to recover on the prescribed medication in your diagnosed mental health problem or need, and you can eventually come off medication. This can be achieved by the right help and guidance from your GP or consultants with the required training.

Comic Relief

Comic Relief spends an amount of time supporting people with mental health issues and increases the availability of the services around the country and the world. It is very important like the country Africa and its people who can develop mental health issues and need help with expressing how quickly the person uses services and resources to aid the recovery process and the person who can tell the person by the first diagnoses of the different mental health issues which people have in their lifetime at any time.

Personal assistants

When a personal assistant has changed mental health from council funded to different ways of providing part of a service and the use of the resources like Pass personal assistant supported services is a way of improving mental health in general and the surrounding areas.

There are different clients with different needs or problems who require the service and who use it each week.

I have gained a lot from a personal assistant already and will improve my own mental health even further and may not require the service in the future as I might gain complete independence, an idea that was first suggested by Dr Tint sometime in the past.

Social services and resources

The use of different social services and resources around the country and the world provide different kinds of services and provision of social services and also buildings with people with mental health needs or problems. They can occur with different situations and during everyday life and they can develop them over a period of time and may need help to start the recovery process when they come out of hospital and go into the community around the country and the world.

People with mental health needs or problems can start to employ a personal assistant if they want to and if they require them. From a council funding their mental health needs or problem by changing the provision of the service they provide over time and eventually gain complete independence from the person who provides the service as mission accomplished. If it can be achieved where possible.

The country

The country and its scenery is very nice and picturesque and you can go for walks in it with your family and friends and also new ones you meet over the years and the countryside has lots of wildlife around it and the trees and plants change over the four seasons, Autumn,Winter, Summer and Spring.

The importance of the environment is essential in keeping nature and humans together and keeping the earth for future generations of people who come into the world.

The country has changed as well with fewer woods and less trees being cut down and future building on housing estates and future planning permission being given or being rejected.

The plants and animals have to adapt to global warming because the weather is changing all over the world.

The countryside improves mental health with people going for walks for exercise each week or weekend in different places around the country and also the world.

Gardens

The uses of gardens first started a long time ago over the centuries and the way gardens were designed by different designers of the layouts of the gardens like Tatton Park in Cheshire.

The gardens were first designed before the hall was even built. They were all important before the big stately homes were even built like Chatsworth House and gardens and other stately homes and displays of the layouts of the gardens and the people who built them and designed them for the Lord or family who owned the estate and gardens.

I really enjoy walking around different gardens around the country and also in different countries of origin. I would like to visit Tunisia to walk around the country and its gardens and parks with family and friends.

Consultants

Consultants, who work with different people in mental health, improve the patients lives and their well being as a whole, or doctors who work in the medicine side of the National Health Service provide good service and national requirement for life. They all help the doctors in their own surgeries and hospitals if the person is required to go into hospital at any time.

People who develop mental health issues or problems can overcome them with help and the experience of the medical staff and people in the community.

They may need help at a certain time and the help is required when the help is in the form the people who are in the caring professions are interested in a career of helping people who are the patients they look after in life and give hours of their time to the job they choose to do.

Harry Potter

It is important to read books like Harry Potter written by JK Rowling. This has been a real success story for her to write the complete series of Harry Potter books and to have films made out of them. Reading books is an important way of improving mental health and bringing people's recovery faster from their mental health need or problem.

A library is a very important place to read. It would be a shame if they eventually close down in the future. You need to learn to read first and continue to be able to read in places where you might not be able to afford a book so that you might be able to read books in a library in Sandbach and Crewe. I first learnt how to read books in the library in Sandbach and Crewe.

Reading is an important way of improving mental health.

Family

We all have family when we are born. It is an essential part of life. You might have some brothers or sisters when you are younger. Your parents bring you up or sometimes give you away when the person is very young or old depending on circumstances. The importance of families in mental health is essential to the recovery process and how quickly the person recovers from their mental health need or problem.

It is important to share and help each other to bring up the persons who have mental health problems or needs when they develop the need over time or stress depending on their mental health or diagnosed mental health needs or problems. They can be helped by medical staff or by talking to each other as a way to improve mental health.

The importance of families can vary sometimes with different backgrounds and people's acceptance of mental health can be put together in a way to funding the services and resources that help the person with a way of improving mental health.

Families combine together as a way of improving mental health needs and problems with the funding of services and resources around the country and also the world.

Yourself and medication

When you first become ill with a prescribed dose of medication for the diagnosed mental health issue need or problem which is given out during the day or at night time. You can eventually take your own medication yourself, but the main point is not to become ill with a mental health issue during your life time. You have the chance to come off medication. It must be taken at the most important time and to make sure it works properly when you are off it but it is all right to still use the service and resources for mental health issues and the experience of medical staff or people in the community and students who learn about mental health but as I have mentioned, it must be yourself in the last printed piece of work to try to make it work to and succeed, or people who know your mental health records at hospital like Leighton and Altrincham Priory or the hospital which looks after you with the diagnosed mental health need or problem.

Carehays Castle

Yesterday we went to a castle near Goran Haven for a walk in its gardens and we took some pictures of the flowers and plants in the garden around the castle. It is important for people with mental health issues to continue going to Cornwall for holidays to improve their mental health issues and to use resources and services around the country and the world.

Different places to visit with different people with mental health issues and the use of resources and services which people provide. The provision and the experience of the medical staff and people in the community and the importance of people with mental health needs, issues, and problems around the country and also the world.

Flats

The importance of Fairburn Avenue in the recovery process in improving mental health are the friends I have made friends with over the last sixteen years, Staff and members who are not part of the service any more or have left for new jobs in their careers who have moved on to new things in their lives. It is important to improve the services and the use of resources which are provided in the improvement of mental health and making new friends at any time of your life and in the future. The importance of travelling to different places to how to improve mental health and the services and resources of mental health centres which provide help for people with mental health issues and the use of the services around the country and also the worlds. The structure of mental health now and in the future could be improved by funding and making sure money is used by making sure that it does not ever come up again as an issue, and people are left to do what they are capable of with help to promote what people with different diagnosed mental health issues can achieve and show the public what can be achieved with help or by themselves and the resources of medical staff and members and future friends I meet in the future.

Concerts

The importance of different artists performing a concert can improve mental health like Take That, Kylie Minogue , Simply Red and the Beatles which can help a person to recover and speed the recovery process by being excited about seeing the different artists perform the concert around the country and the world. The concerts can help to improve mental health in general.

Working with people with mental health issues

People can make friends with a person with a mental health issue and improve their own lives as well by getting the best out of them and using their experience to improve the job and the place where they work and help to provide mental health help by providing places to go like services and resources around the country and also the world.

You may meet a person with a mental health issue at any time in your life and make friends with them and be aware of mental health issues for the first time and you may like to join them at the centres and talk to them and take them to different places around the country and abroad, and keep in touch with them. Working with a person with mental health issues improves mental health in general, around the country and the world.

Providing services and resources

Mental health needs more funding and the use of services and resources around the country and the world. To meet a person with different mental health issues can help the funding by making the public aware of mental health issues and also being aware that it could happen to themselves at any time, including the person who is helping to provide the help of the services and resources in the job which the person is doing.

Providing services and resources is very important to promote mental health in general and make the public aware of mental health issues needs or problems which they themselves can help by talking to them to make friends and help to improve mental health.

Moving the mental health unit

Moving the mental health unit to Macclesfield from Leighton is not a very good idea because of more petrol for families and friends to visit the person with mental health issues. It is more expensive with more miles to travel than at Crewe. Leighton is where I was born and the services and resources were much better than at Macclesfield hospital. People with mental health issues prefer to be near family and friends when they come out of hospital and start to use the services and resources near their home around the country and the world, in case they are needed, at any time.

Write up on roadmap away from difficulties

A person is anxious who looks after her husband who has a metal health issue and also looked after her two young children. She eventually joined a charity called the Wellbeing project which is a charity which provides help with family issues with depression and anxiety which can happen to anyone at any time, and the services provided for the two main issues mentioned help her to cope with the situation of looking after her family and cope with mental health issues of depression and anxiety which can help to improve mental health in general. And the use of the services available to them as the charity Wellbeing provides help and guidance with the two issues together and the way to use the services and help them in Norfolk and the surrounding area and also provide help with her children when the parent comes across mental health services and uses them to help and improve mental health and her own situation and the two issues together combined with looking after her family. Wellbeing charity receives referrals to sort out the situations which the person requires; the help and guidance of the person who has the experience of the services and resources of the charity provides help and places to talk about the two issues which Cath Parker has come across and experienced. Depression and anxiety combined. People with mental health issues can help to improve the above mentioned subject by services and resources and other services around the country, not just in Norfok. The Wellbeing charity provides help and reassurance to Cath and her family and her two children and can inspire ways of improving mental health in general. In the case of my own mental health issue, depression, combining the two main issues together helps improve mental health.

Depression: improving mental health

When people first become ill at any time with the mental health issue depression like myself and have recovered from it my own experience of it has given me the ability to write my book on how to improve mental health and be an author and write books now and in the future. Depression can be overcome with the right medication. Some people can come off the medication prescribed or if not be on as little as possible but enough to keep them well. But as I have mentioned before it must be you who makes sure it succeeds when the chance is ever given at all by the consultants who look after your mental health issue or needs, and you must show the ability to inspire people with mental health issues or needs and make friends with people who have not experienced it at all and you must also use the services and resources across the country and the world to improve mental health and the mental health issue depression and help to fund other mental health issues in different parts of the country and the world. In general and also help the National Health Service to fund mental health services and resources.

Pop artists and the music industry

The music industry and different artists can develop different mental health issues and may require help from the services and the use of the resources around the country and the world different artists like Adam Ant and several others in the past or in the future as well.

The music industry can be aware and help with the awareness of mental health issues and promote in a way to improve mental health like signal 1 and 2 needs, issues, or problems and help improve mental health in general and the use of the services and resources around the country and the world.

The radio DJ can help to improve mental health by putting songs or compact discs by making a song to promote mental health and recording it in a recording studio, selling it to raise money for mental health for services and resources in the local area, and the surrounding areas.

A song to improve mental health

One day in the life of a person with a mental health issue uses the sea, sand, beaches, and the seaside and places around the country and the world to help promote mental health and services and the use of resources in hospitals and in the community. Like the charity Mind which helps people with mental health issues, Leighton Hospital in Crewe and now in Macclesfield. When you require the help and in a friendly way and use the experience of the medical staff, patients, community, people, residents and other hospitals with mental health units and funding and resources and services around the country and the world using pets that people have, listening to birds and the waves of the sea and different ways of improving mental health as well.

The way to sing a song about mental health and promote is to advertise it and go to a recording studio and get permission and gain the help of certain people in the music industry and sing it together and record it and try to sell it in the top 40 charts, and raise money for mental health services and resources in the local area and the surrounding areas.

The National Health Service

The National Health Service was formed in 1948 to provide mental health provision and services and resources and training for doctors and nurses around the country and the world to help in emergencies when required and the guidance of the medical staff and also in the community like community nurses who go to different people's houses to help provide help when needed.

The National Health Service is an important national health asset to the country and also the world, which helps to promote mental health and also to improve it as well. The services and resources around the country and the world, and the provision and training required each year, as well as world mental health day.

The future

When the National Health Service receives enough funding to fund all its services and resources and is really appreciated by whatever Government is in power and is properly funded mental health services and resources around the country and the world and the help of the medical staff is given enough money to live on and is funded is found for the services and resources which people use in the National Health Service, a national asset to the country and also the world when they tour Britain. And visit our national heritage sites around the country, when required or needed. In hospitals and around the country.

It is great to improve mental health and the use of its services and resources in different places like Crewe, Stoke and London which provide hospitals for all of us to use if needed.

My own idea is to make sure that mental health is properly funded to provide services and resources that everyone can use in any situation and learn about mental health in your life. You can make friends with a person with a mental health issue and they may know how to achieve the best results depending on experience and the way to use the services and resources around the country and also the world and ability to make friends with people who have not had any experience of mental health issues, needs or problems which people can require help from the services and members who have experienced it during their time were ill with the different diagnosed mental health issues.

Football on prescription

When I first started playing football again on Crewe Alexandra training ground and also in Legends in the winter I really enjoyed playing the game again. I was really improving my football as I used to play it with my best friend Peter Williams at Elworth Primary School, and also with my friends I used to go to school with. It is an important way to improve mental health in general and in the world.

Leighton hospital

The queen first opened Leighton in 1972. It has provided mental health help for 36 years. It was a great idea for it to open in 1972; a great new hospital to provide mental health provision and services and resources. It is a great shame to move the mental health unit to Macclesfield.

The nurses provide the time and care in their career they choose. Leighton hospital has provided a good place for me to recover from my diagnosed mental health issue, which is depression.

Macclesfield mental health unit

It is a real shame to move the mental health unit from Crewe Leighton Hospital after so many years since it was opened by the queen in 1972. The move of the mental health unit from Leighton Hospital to Macclesfield is a change for the worse because of more money for transport for family members to see the patients in Macclesfield hospital.

Socialising improving mental health

People go socialising to the pub and to other places around the country like gardens and stately homes like the National Trust, like places to visit like Taton Park, Lyme Park and other National Trust properties around the country and the world.

Improving mental health is very important to promote mental health issues services and resources around the country and also the world. The National Health Service is a great asset to the country when needed. Socialising with people with mental health issues is very important way of improving mental health services and resources like Crewe and Nantwich, a great way of improving mental health issues, needs or problems when they occur in life.

Socialising is an important way of improving mental health in general.

Different ways of improving mental health

The ways of improving mental health are services, resources and the use of them by the patient, the person in the community and the future person in the service and the use of the resources available to them at present and in the future as well.

Different ways of improving mental health in general are by music, relaxation, and the use of art in relaxing a person to express their way of improving their mental health in general and the future.

The ways of national integration of mental health are a very important part of improving mental health around the world and the country, and the future of mental health in general and the use of the patient person in the community, the medical staff who work in the mental health units in different hospitals around the world and the country as well.

Macon House improving mental health

The services and resources and building Macon House is an important way of improving mental health and the use of services and resources and social services around the country and the world.

Macon House is a very important way of improving mental health in general as well as the members of staff and medical staff who provide the provision for the services and resources around the country.

291 Nantwich road

The use of 291 in improving mental health is a very important way of improving mental health in general and the future as well as in the past. Working with other people with mental health issues and the use of the services and resources available to them and members staff combine together in defeating mental health and the stigma a well as proving to the general public that it can be dealt with in a suitable way to improve mental health, from the beginning when it was first started to the present day and in the future.

Services and resources in mental health

The process of services and resources in mental health are the provision of services members and staff working together to promote mental health and the combining them together, working with medical staff and members patients and people in the community using the services and resources to work together to improve mental health in general the medical staff members and people who specialise in the area of caring and the professions the National Health Service. Services and resources combining together to promote mental health and improve the service and the use of resources around the country and the world.

The use of services and mental health buildings to improve the service as a whole and the general outlook of mental health services and resources together combining with people with mental health issues needs or problems can overcome with help from professionals who work in mental health with the medical staff members patients and people in the community.

The use of buildings

The use of mental health buildings to improve mental health like Macon House, 291 Nantwich Road South Cheshire College helps to promote positive images of mental health and their uses of the services and resources that help to promote people working together and team building to promote the uses of the combining of mental health in general and the future.

The buildings I have mentioned have really helped me to improve my mental health and gave me the inspiration to write my book called How to improve mental health. And the future of the service and the use of resources around the country and also the world. To make sure that mental health issues do not exist any more. The buildings have improved mental health in general immensely and

291 is not needed any more as it is surplus to requirements. A real shame.

Mill House

The use of Mill House really helps to promote mental health and the use of the bistro to raise the issues of mental health and the residents staff and people who work in the bistro combine together to show the public how mental health and ordinary people can work together to promote mental health and improve the service as a whole. Mill House is a very good way to improve mental health. It brings more confidence to get to know the residents who live at Mill House and people who work there.

Summary

The book How to Improve Mental Health is aimed at patients, medical staff, people in the community and services and resources to improve mental health around the country and also the world. It is meant to help the public understand more about mental health, an issue that may affect us all at some time in our own lives at any time. To promote the services and resources which people can access if they ever come across a diagnosis of a mental health issue and know how to use the services and resources available to them when required or needed, but if you can avoid getting ill at all it would be better for you as a whole during your life time, to help people with mental health issue to also show how to recover from their own diagnosed mental health issue as well as my own diagnosed mental health issue, depression.

This book is written by Tim Price as a thank you for the use of mental health services and resources over the last 21 years. To help and inspire other people with mental health issues and to show how the recovery process is used to improve mental health and the combining of the services resources, professionals, and people in the community and to help promote mental health and the recovery process.

I am going to continue to write more books because I want to become an author as a part time job.